# WILD STORIES

## Proof That God Cares About the Details Of Your Life

By Jill Bowman

Dedication

To the Creator of Wild Stories:
May people have eyes to see
and ears to hear what You are
doing in their midst, so that they
will know and trust Your heart,
stand in awe of Your creative power,
give You all the glory,
and gain joy and fulfillment
beyond their wildest dreams.

# Contents


Why Stories?........................................................1
An Unlikely Witness................................................4
Leading by Following..............................................11
Falling Into Grace................................................15
Fearfully and Wonderfully Made....................................18
Divine Appointments...............................................22
I Am Second.......................................................25
Angels Watching Over Me...........................................29
American Miracles.................................................31
Close to the Brokenhearted........................................37
#LetUsWorship.....................................................39
Full Reliance.....................................................44
Nazi Survivor.....................................................48
Day One...........................................................55
What Difference Does It Make?.....................................58
Mission: Possible.................................................63
Prayer for Salvation..............................................65

# Why Stories?

What is it about stories? They grab our attention, pull us in. A good story can make us stay up all night, reading a book to the last page, or binge-watching episodes of a TV series until we get to the very end!

When we meet a person, how do we get to know them? By hearing the story of their life: where they were born, where they grew up, what their life was like, the choices they made and what happened next.

What is it that makes people get so excited about their favorite sports team? When they talk about the big game last weekend, with all of its triumphs and tragedies, its heroes and its villains, they are telling a story.

Isn't it true that all the most well-loved stories have some things in common? Things like love, romance, danger, adventure, betrayal, and redemption. Great stories will have a victorious ending, or one in which complete tragedy was averted through heroic sacrifice. How is it that these same elements can yield countless stories that grab the attention of audiences everywhere? The billions of dollars spent each year on entertainment, proliferation of streaming services like Netflix and Amazon Prime, and the popularity of story-based video games are all evidence of our unending thirst for a good story.

This truth first hit home to me thanks to its eloquent revelation by John Eldredge in his book Epic. He writes that stories move us so deeply because they tell us something about our lives, our hearts. I highly recommend his inspiring exploration of the idea that we are living in an epic story, and that we each have a crucial role to play.

In my first book, This Is Not Heaven, I added a chapter titled Wild Stories almost as an afterthought. After all, the book wasn't supposed to be about me. It was supposed to provide some practical steps to take, moment by moment, on order to move toward a life that was full of energy and hope. But in the days since it was published, I've been realizing how much energy and hope I've gained from hearing the "wild stories" of other people throughout my life. In truth, I can't imagine what my life would look like without hearing these stories. They have shown me the way toward this life of energy and hope I have found. I have gained courage, determination, strength, and faith from hearing them, which I have needed at crucial moments in my life.

For example, when I was a young woman, I had an oversized fear of being the victim of rape. I felt vulnerable, and weak. I doubted my ability to defend myself. But one day I heard an interview of Margy Mayfield who was forced at gunpoint to drive out of a parking lot with a man she suspected was a serial rapist on the run from authorities. Hearing her recount every gripping detail of her story of being abducted by Stephen Morin changed my life. I wanted what she had that got her through that ordeal.

She described the moment he forced his way into her car. She realized this was likely the man being hunted by police, and yet she was not terrified. She felt a peace that she knew was from God. She was concerned for her own safety, but she stepped into trust that God had allowed this moment, and she decided to allow God to use her that day. She spent ten hours with Stephen Morin before he finally surrendered himself to police. Margy Mayfield was unharmed.

This is just one of many, many true stories that have come to my mind in moments when I needed courage, compassion, patience, humility, strength...you name it. It's one thing to have read in the bible that "God is with us" and "God is our refuge." But when I hear the true stories of people who have actually been protected by and provided for by God, I find real-life mentors and examples to follow in life. Their stories give me the faith and courage I need to, as Dr. Charles Stanley says, "obey God, and leave all the consequences to him." When facing a challenge, I can talk to God about it, see it from his perspective, and face it with confidence, giving my all without becoming overwhelmed.

A note about skepticism: some of the stories you are about to read will probably seem unbelievable. Go ahead, be skeptical! It's wise to be discerning. If you pay close attention, you'll start to see patterns, as I have, through years of listening to people's stories about how God stepped into their circumstances and did something wild. I have seen how their stories echo certain themes, themes that can also be found in the stories of people in the bible. I have learned things about the One who is stepping in and making a difference in people's lives. The stories in these pages have been selected because they reflect those patterns.

It is my hope that your life will be enriched by these stories, as mine has. Enjoy!

# An Unlikely Witness

When skeptics hear the outlandish stories of people claiming miracles, they naturally think these people are just desperately trying to gain fame and fortune by making up a story that will sell. But skeptics would hardly be able to claim that profile of Dr. Mary C. Neal. In fact, she avoided telling her story for ten years, even though that was exactly the assignment she was given when it happened to her.

I first heard the story of Dr. Mary Neal on The Eric Metaxas Show. Her interview can be heard on his YouTube channel. It is titled The Eric Metaxas Show: Dr. Mary Neal (Part 1). The second half of the interview is titled The Eric Metaxas Show: Dr. Mary Neal (Part 2).

Dr. Neal was a successful orthopedic surgeon in Jackson Hole, Wyoming. She was a wife, a mother of three young boys, and in hindsight, a self-described "nominal Christian." She and her husband were avid kayakers.

On the last day of a kayaking trip in Chile, a challenging river with several waterfalls was their destination. The navigation of one of the falls did not go as planned, and Dr. Neal's kayak became lodged in the rocks below, pinning her under 8 feet of water, where she realized she would drown. She remembers thinking that she had always expected she could drown while kayaking, and she had imagined it would be terrifying. But in this moment, she felt peaceful.

"I experienced no air hunger, no pain, no panic, no fear. I began to calmly pray. Oddly, I didn't pray for God to rescue me. Instead, I prayed only, "Your will be done." It wasn't about giving up. It was more about actively turning toward God. That's why I often say that God didn't take my future—I willingly gave it to him."

In her second book, 7 Lessons from Heaven, she describes "the physical sensation of being held and comforted by Jesus, as tangibly as I could feel the plastic of the boat around my body and the weight of the water pressing on my torso." She says that time seemed to stop. Jesus assured her that everything was fine, that her family would be fine. She felt his boundless love, kindness, compassion, and mercy. He showed her the story of her life, including some good memories, and some of memories of painful interactions with people close to her. Through these memories, Jesus reminded her "of the great beauty that comes of all events." (This idea is echoed in Paul's words in Romans 8:28, that "all things work together for the good of those who love God and are called according to his purpose.")

She goes on to describe the sensation of leaving her body, and of being greeted by people in heaven who knew her and loved her. She experienced pure love, immeasurable kindness and generosity, indescribable beauty, infinite mercy and grace. Jesus reviewed with her the events of her life. She was shown times that she had been hurt by people. In those times, she was able to see the event from the other person's perspective. She understood what had brought them to that moment. She felt love and compassion for them, and forgiveness came easily. She understood, too, that she was forgiven for the times when she had hurt others.

But she was disappointed to learn that her time on earth was not done. She was told that her nine-year-old son would die "soon", and that she was to use her own near-death experience to help others see the beauty of his life and of his death. When she asked brokenheartedly, "Why my son?" she was immediately reminded of Jesus' promise to her that she could "always count on God's love, and trust that his plan for each person, and for the world, is one of hope."

Within 15 minutes of her kayak becoming stuck under the water, Dr. Neal's friends found her. They began CPR. After 30 minutes of unconsciousness, she began to breathe again. Their next task was to get her broken body out of that remote river valley and into a hospital.  Out of nowhere, two Chilean men appeared. The men helped to put her into a boat and carry her up the hillside, clearing the brush with a machete. The journey was long and difficult. Both of her knees were broken, yet she felt no pain during the entire journey. After several hours of carrying her up hillsides, they emerged onto a dirt road. Miraculously, there was an ambulance waiting. They loaded her into the ambulance and travelled several hours to a medical outpost for help. Afterwards, her friends travelled back to the river to find out more about the two men who helped them, and about the ambulance. The local people did not know of the men they described, and there was no such thing as an ambulance in the area.

Dr. Neal spent the first few months of her recovery using all of her medical knowledge and scientific reasoning to disprove her experience. She was highly motivated; if she could disprove what she had experienced, she could let go of her mandate to tell others, and she could disregard the idea that her son would die "soon". In Chapter 5 of 7 Lessons from Heaven, she details all the possible alternatives she explored. Ultimately, she concluded that what she experienced was real, and she needed to share her story, and brace herself for the tragedy that was to come.

For several years she carried the burden alone, not telling anyone. She treasured every moment, not only with her oldest son, but with everyone she loved. As the years passed, she grew concerned that it was not fair to carry this knowledge alone, since it had given her a perspective that enabled her to potentially face the future in a way that she would have few regrets. She decided to tell her husband. Together they agreed that this was too great a load for a young man to carry, so they waited to tell their son until his eighteenth birthday.

In the early morning hours of that day in 2007, she was filled with emotion. Her precious son was alive! She tearfully told him about her near death experience and what she had been told. He listened attentively, but gave no hint of his own thoughts on the matter. Later that day, he had a brief conversation with his father about what she had told him. After that, it was not discussed again.

In the coming days and weeks, as her son continued to live on and plan for his future, she began to believe that God's plans had changed. She began to relax and focus on enjoying the rest of their lives.

One thing remained, hanging over her head like a black cloud: she knew she needed to write a book about her experience. The thoughts of inadequacy for the task and ideas about the large amount of time it would take persisted, until one morning in the spring of 2009, when she awoke with a small flash of desire to start writing. She wrestled with her doubts, and her reluctance finally vanished.

Writing about her experiences was exhilarating. For many years, she had avoided dwelling on what had happened to her in order to do what she had needed to do every day. Now that she was writing about what happened, she allowed herself to fully relive all that she had experienced. On June 21ˢᵗ, she hit "Save" for what she thought would be the last time, and her spirit soared. She had finally done what God had asked of her. She had written her first book, To Heaven and Back.

Amazingly, the tremendous joy of that moment would give way to deep sorrow only hours later, when the family learned that their oldest son had just been hit by a car and killed.

The Neal family was devastated. In Chapter 12 of 7 Lessons from Heaven, she recounts the many facets of their grief, and how each person in the family experienced grief differently. She also describes some of the actions they took that helped them in the aftermath. I highly recommend this chapter to those who have experienced a difficult loss.

Today, Dr. Neal counts it a privilege to speak with people about their life stories. She says in her interview with Eric Metaxas, "Everyone is worried about the same thing. Everyone has regrets from their past. Everyone has anxiety about their future. Everyone is going to face challenges. Everyone is so afraid of dying that so many people never [choose to] actually live.

"We aren't here to live an easy life. None of us ever change without a challenge. We will change in response to the challenges that we've faced. My passion currently is to help people face those challenges from a state of joy. So many of us seek happiness, based on our external circumstances. I believe that joy is based on an absolute trust in the promises of God, regardless of our circumstances. He is real and present. He knows us each as individuals, loving us each as if we were the only one. Trust in God is based on evidence. I challenge people to prove me wrong, because I absolutely know that if people will take the time and put out the effort to truthfully look at their own life, they will absolutely see evidence of God's presence, evidence that can't be made up.

"One of the problems with our culture is that we are constantly presented with the false choice of belief in science or belief in God and spirituality. Science will always be the means by which we try to understand how things happen, but spirituality will always provide the answer to why, and they coexist very easily, and they should coexist in every person's life. We are given the gift of intellectual curiosity, and we should question things. At the same time, we also can't discount everything. Not everything is a miracle, but the fact is there are miracles. Choosing to believe God's promises is transformational.

"Believing God's promises on a daily basis radically changes human interaction. If I come across someone I don't like, I can immediately remind myself that they are as intensely loved by God as I know God loves me, and that changes how I experience them. I try to look for God within them, I try to feel love for them. Where God's love is present, there is no room for destructive emotion, and so all of a sudden, I start to like them. All of a sudden, it's not 'me versus them', it's 'us'. If someone hurts me, I don't feel anger or resentment. I can look at them and trust that they have a life story that brought them to that point, and I can forgive them. Believing God's promises changes my experience of life. I can only imagine for a moment if everyone on the earth were able to actually accept the intensity of God's love for them, and reflect that to other people, oh my goodness, we'd obviously have a very different world."

I call Dr. Neal an unlikely witness because she wasn't looking for anything in her life to change. She had all that most people hope for in life. But in one day, the truth of God's promises became real to her, and she realized there was undeniably so much more to life than she had known before.

**Challenges:** Take some time to recall some of the pivotal moments of your past, and look for evidence of God's presence. Think about a difficult person in your life, and imagine them from God's perspective.

# Leading by Following

One person who has had a huge influence on my faith is Dr. Charles Stanley. He is the pastor of First Baptist Church in Atlanta, and leader of InTouch Ministries (intouch.org). As TV pastors go, he is one that stands above the rest.

This man is not a showman, waving his arms and speaking in a thundering voice, hoping to spur his viewers to give offerings to his ministry. Dr. Stanley's voice instead reflects the peace and joy that is the fruit of a life placed in the trustworthy hands of Almighty God.

Through the many years I've listen to Dr. Stanley's messages, I have learned much.  The real-life examples he uses to illustrate biblical attitudes and actions have been life-changing for me.

One of his stories that has inspired me was the story of how he came to be president of the Southern Baptist Convention. The time had come for the current president to step down, and the leaders were meeting to select the next president. Dr. Stanley was in a pastoral position at the time that was very stable, and he was not interested in being considered for this new role, but was participating in the meetings for the purpose of praying with everyone in order to seek God's direction and leadership in who the new president should be. One morning, as he was about to leave his hotel room to join the day's meetings, he says he heard God saying, "Don't touch that doorknob until you are ready to accept this position." He says he had a very serious conversation with God for the next few minutes, but eventually accepted. In the role, God provided resources in the areas that Dr. Stanley had concerns about, and used the position to grow his faith. When a person steps out in faith, knowing that God is calling them to do something even though they don't feel equipped to do it, God is faithful to honor that obedience and he provides in amazing ways!

Another story that has inspired me was the story he tells about the church moving to a new property. It was apparent that the church was growing and needed to find a new location. The leadership prayed and felt the Lord leading them to purchase a particular property. They entered negotiations with the owner, but those negotiations stalled. The leadership continued to pray and ask for direction. In their prayer time, they felt led that this property was the one, and that the Lord wanted them to pray for it in the way that the Israelites prayed for Jericho. If you know the story, you know that this required the bold act of walking around the property once a day for six days, praying and singing to the Lord. On the seventh day, it required that bold act to be repeated seven times! This was an unusual requirement, but the leadership decided that they would faithfully follow through with this act. Amazingly, the day after this act was completed, the owner of the property called and was ready to sell! My takeaway from this story, and from many stories in the bible like it, is that sometimes God will ask us to do something that makes no sense to us as an opportunity to step out in faith.

On the InTouch website, on a page titled "Life Principle 23: You Can Never Outgive God," Dr. Stanley writes another personal story about joining God in the work that he is doing. Dr.

Stanley tells the story of a time that the church was raising funds for an expansion project. He prayed specifically that God would show him what he should contribute personally. He had already given to the project, but he sensed God was requiring something more. Soon, he felt God impressing upon him to give his camera equipment. Since photography was Dr. Stanley's favorite hobby, this was a painful request! "However," he writes, "God's conviction was strong and to the point. There was no way I wanted to avoid making the right decision. I knew that my obedience would lead to blessing. If He wanted my cameras, I wanted to give them to Him. After all, He owned them anyway."

He continues, "A few days later, I sold my equipment and gave the money to the building fund. Many other members of our congregation also gave personal possessions and treasures. It was a great time in our fellowship for seeking God's will with our finances and also allowing Him to prove His faithfulness to each one of us. When it came time to sign the paperwork for our new property, we had the money we needed and did not have to borrow a single penny."

"Several months later, a woman rang my doorbell. When I opened it, I noticed she had two very large shopping bags. She asked, "Are you Charles Stanley?" I didn't know what to think but I replied, "Yes, I am." Then she said, "This is for you." She set the bags down and walked away. I looked inside one of them and immediately recognized my camera equipment. God had returned every lens and every camera body to me. Is this the way He works? I believe it is. Many times, He tests us to see where our true devotion is located. Is it in "things" or is it in Him?"

The InTouch Ministries YouTube channel is filled with messages by Dr. Charles Stanley on so many wonderful topics. Some titles I see right now as I open the YouTube app are "Our Anchor in Times of Storm", "Resting in the Faithfulness of God",

"Walking in the Holy Spirit", "When Opportunities Appear", and "The Awareness of God's Presence." Listening to these messages has helped me to know God better, and understand how he operates and what he cares about. I highly recommend them!

He has also written many books. One of my favorites is 30 Life Principles. All 30 of these biblical principles have something to help us remember in times of difficulty or crisis, which, to be honest, is when we really need to hear a principle that will guide our actions and attitudes. The first principle is "Our intimacy with God – His highest priority for our lives – determines the impact of our lives." The second principle is "Obey God and leave all the consequences to him." The third principle is "God's word is an immovable anchor in times of storm." Another one of my other favorites is the seventh, "The dark moments in our life will only last so long as is necessary for God to accomplish His purpose in us."

I'm so thankful for these resources that are always available to encourage and guide me, especially now that Dr. Stanley has announced his retirement. His videos and books are full of insights into how God works in our world, and timeless practical advice on how to walk in step with God each day.

**Challenge:** Listen to a YouTube video of a message of Dr. Charles Stanley, or visit the InTouch Ministries website. Be ready to take a screen shot or write down something that inspires you, or a practical habit you can start. He WILL say something you'll want to remember!

# Falling Into Grace

I met Lynda at work. Her smiling face and "Awesome day! God bless you!" are experienced daily by those who call in or visit our company. After a few months and a few lunch time conversations with her, I said, "Anyone with your enthusiasm for people must have a story to tell." Soon we became friends, and she told me of her difficult first marriage, and her gratitude for her life now.

A few years ago, Lynda's mother passed, after years spent in a nursing home. Lynda had been spending many hours with her mother each week, making sure she was cared for, tucking her in at night. Suddenly there was a gaping void in Lynda's schedule, which she filled by working more hours at her second job and by working out at a gym. For months and months, she kept busy, numbing herself with activity, running from down time, not wanting to think, not wanting to feel, not wanting to face how much she missed her mom, not wanting to think about she no longer had family nearby, not wanting to lose control. But all of that changed in a moment.

One morning at her second job, she fell from a ladder and shattered the lower vertebrae of her back. Upon admission to the hospital, she was placed in the very hospital room her mother had stayed. Lynda fought the memories of her mother's painful struggle through life with two rods and multiple screws in her back, fearing the same fate, and facing it all alone.

"At first I fought what was happening to me. I was in so much pain, but I refused the pain medication that my mother had taken because I didn't want my body to get used to it. I refused a catheter because I didn't want to accept that I needed to be stuck in my bed. Then an angel appeared in the corner of my room. She looked like my mom. She said, 'Come on, Sis. You can do this.' I was shocked, then calmed. I was able to accept that what was happening to me was terrible, but I would be okay."

Then Lynda's new reality began to sink in. Day after day, friends came to visit, bringing flowers and cards and gifts. People whose lives Lynda had touched came to touch hers. They kept coming in the weeks following surgery, kept coming during the weeks in the transitional care unit, and finally in the weeks still recovering at home. They helped with her dogs and her car, ran errands, organized and helped to fill out paperwork, but most of all, they acted like family.

Through it all, Lynda began to see God moving through her circumstances, and she knew she was in his trustworthy hands. So many of her doctors and nurses and other people caring for her were also believers in Christ. They encouraged her in what she thought was already her strong faith. Little had she known she had been hesitating to fully trust. But now, when she could not do anything for herself, she found that he was there, surrounding her with people who were ready to be the hands and feet of Jesus for her. She learned that she was not in control, but that was okay, because when she thanked him for what she had, and asked for what she needed, her prayers were being answered!

Today, Lynda's days (and nights) are still impacted by a significant level of pain. Still, she counts herself blessed that things happened the way they did. "The fifty-pound box I was lifting fell on me. I was told that if I had fallen an eighth of an inch to the right I would have been paralyzed, and an eighth of an inch to the left I would have hit my head and I'd have been dead. Also, the baker forgot something and came back into the freezer five minutes after I fell. I could have been in there for who knows how long."

In spite of the daily pain she experiences, Lynda would not trade the depth of meaning her life and her relationships have gained. She is filled with hope, drawing on God's strength when she is weak, and praising him for all he has done, that only he could do!

Lynda's life verse: "For I know the plans I have for you," declares the Lord, "plans to prosper you and not to harm you, plans to give you a future and a hope." (Jeremiah 29:11)

**Challenge:** Think of a struggle you have that most people don't have to deal with. God could be using that struggle to make you more aware of his presence and his ability to provide for you. Bring it to him and see what happens.

# Fearfully and Wonderfully Made

I met Allison at work when she was in college. It was so wonderful to see this beautiful, soft-spoken young woman every day as she made plans for her bright future. I had the opportunity as well to meet her handsome college sweetheart that would become her husband.

In time I moved away, but social media made it easy to stay in touch. It was a joy to see pictures of Allison and Eric's wedding and their growing family. Little did they know they would soon face a serious health concern. Allison shared their story in the comments of the Facebook Virtual Book Signing event for my first book, This Is Not Heaven. With her permission, I'm sharing them with you here.

"When I was 20 weeks pregnant with our third child, we received the devastating news that she had a severe form of spina bifida. We were told that there was a surgery available that could be done to repair her spine while she was still in the womb. It was a risky surgery for both me and the baby and while it didn't cure the spina bifida it could lessen the damages of the condition. But the surgery could also cause the need for the baby to be delivered immediately which she would not survive. We already had two other small children. My husband and I would have to travel to another state for the surgery and I would have to be away from my family for the remainder of the pregnancy. It was the biggest decision that I had ever faced in my life and we would have to decide in a few short days.

"During that time, I couldn't sleep at night because the stress of the decision was causing this constant audible chaos in my brain. Whenever I fell asleep, the noise would immediately wake me up. I had never experienced anything like it. One night, after begging and pleading with God to help us make the right decision I suddenly felt Him urging me to pursue the fetal surgery. Immediately, the noise in my head stopped and I felt relaxed for the first time in days. It was so clear to me what we needed to do. The surgery was a success and today my daughter, Faith, is a living, breathing, walking miracle of a 4-year-old!"

Faith's medical challenges have required much of each member of the family. From extra time and patience needed to accommodate Faith's mobility, to time away from each other for medical appointments and surgeries, each member of their family has had ample opportunities to develop patience, kindness, generosity, and determination. They do their best to make the most of their time together, always looking for new places to slowly explore and fully appreciate. Allison spoke a little more about this in a recent email with me, which she also has allowed me to share.

"When we were first given her spina bifida diagnosis, I felt like my life was over. It seemed like it would be such a burden to care for a child with special needs. I thought our whole family would suffer and I couldn't see how anything would ever be 'normal' again. What I couldn't see at that time was how much of a joy she would be and how incredible it would be to see her overcome any challenge that she encounters. I didn't know that her sweet and affectionate personality would brighten any room that she enters. I couldn't look ahead to understand that any difficulty that we would face would be completely worth it for this amazing little girl.

"I think the biggest lesson that the Lord has taught me (and is often still teaching me) is that He has a perfect and wonderful plan for our lives, even when things look very discouraging on the surface. When Faith was 2 years old, she required another surgery on her back, this time to repair a tethered spinal cord.  It's known to be a painful surgery and the recovery is not easy since it requires the person to lay flat on their back for three weeks while the incision heals.  Keep in mind, Faith was 2 years old during the time of her surgery which is a particularly active age! There was also the possibility that the surgery could cause Faith to lose the function in her legs that she had worked so hard at achieving through daily physical therapy. The surgery went well, though. Faith didn't lose any function in her body and she made it through the difficult time of not being able to do much aside from laying on the couch. We were so thankful! Then, out of nowhere, the month after her surgery, we were shocked to find out that Faith had broken her leg, most likely in a fall from her walker. Then, a few months later, another broken leg and then a broken ankle too. We were devastated to learn that Faith's 3 weeks of laying on the couch for the surgery recovery had caused her bones (which are already weakened from spina bifida) to be further weakened and very prone to fracture. Each of those fractures had a profound impact on Faith's mobility. They changed the shape and angle of her bones causing her additional challenges relating to walking.

"I remember it as such a discouraging time. During the 2-hour drive to the Children's Hospital ER for the third fracture, I remember confessing my discouragement to God.  I felt Him responding to me that it was okay to be discouraged but to remember that He has plans to use this for His glory.

"Faith kept striving along, even after a major surgery and three separate fractures. She was determined to be stronger than ever and she learned to work through the adversity. She has worked so hard and now she is walking more independently than she ever has. She no longer needs a walker all the time, she can now walk with crutches and sometimes just one crutch.

"Faith inspires me to try to look past the current obstacle that I may be facing at that time and remember that God has a plan for it and He is using it to make us stronger and allow us to trust more fully in Him."

Living with spina bifida requires vigilance and careful management of a variety of possible symptoms. It would be easy for parents to feel overwhelmed by things they can't control. But Allison has learned to trust that God will lead them, and he will provide what they need. Walking with him through every new challenge enables Allison to see life not as a treacherous journey, but rather a glorious adventure where painful moments will pass, and there will be wonderful moments ahead to celebrate victories and blessings.

For you created my inmost being; you knit me together in my mother's womb. I praise you because I am fearfully and wonderfully made. (Psalm 139:13-14a)

**Challenge:** Is there an obstacle in your life that is causing you to move forward more slowly in life than you would like? List some possible benefits that God might be providing to you through the slower pace you are being forced to keep.

# Divine Appointments

Nik Ripken, in his book The Insanity of God, shares many stories of his adventures in serving God in nations where Christianity is seen as a threat to the local and national authorities. The book is full of stories of divine appointments that only God could have arranged.

My favorite is the story of a doctor who kept emailing Nik to urgently come to his country. Nik kept replying that his current trip with multiple destinations had already been tightly arranged, and that he would be coming to that area the following year. But when two consecutive legs of his journey had to be rescheduled due to illness and imprisonment of the people he planned to visit, Nik realized that he was suddenly available.

Upon arriving at the airport, he met the doctor, who was standing next to five men in traditional Muslim dress that were looking at Nik attentively.

"Who are your friends?" said Nik.

"You don't know who they are?" the doctor asked.

"No, I didn't even know who you were until thirty seconds ago," said Nik.

"Well, Dr. Ripken, if you don't know them, and I don't know them, we have a serious security problem. They told me that they had come to meet you. I'm going to have to leave you now. Here's my cell phone number. Call me if everything turns out alright, and I will come back and get you."

Nik realized he could be in danger. He casually headed toward the terminal to see if he could catch a flight out. But the men followed him. They tugged at his clothes to get him to stop. Finally, in broken English they said, "Please stop, sir. We are followers of Jesus."

Still wary, but sensing God's hand on their meeting, he went with them to a small apartment. They all sat on the floor. The men smiled at him and waited for him to speak. He told them a little bit about himself, how he had been traveling around the world, doing research, and speaking to believers in Jesus in different parts of the world. The men began to laugh. Then they explained.

These five men had come to know each other because they had each miraculously received bibles through unusual circumstances, had read them, and decided to follow Jesus. One man had dreamt about meeting Jesus, then was approached in the market the next day by a stranger who said, "The Holy Spirit told me to give you this book." Another dreamt of a blue book, and was told in the dream to search for it. He searched and searched until one day he found it in a Quranic book shop, printed in his own language.

All five of the men had been rejected by their families and friends after becoming believers in Jesus. They had all fled their country and had come to know one another in this small border town. For two months, they had been praying from midnight to three in the morning for someone to come to tell them how to follow Jesus. They said, "We prayed for someone who knows about persecution, someone who knows what other believers are doing, someone who can encourage and teach us. At 1:30 this morning, the Holy Spirit told us to go to the airport and go to the first white man that comes off the plane. The Holy Spirit told us that He was sending this man to answer our questions."

The many stories like this retold in The Insanity of God encourage me that God can reach anyone, anywhere, even if they are all alone. God is weaving incredible stories of redemption and rescue in the world today. As 2 Chronicles 16:9 says, "For the eyes of the Lord run to and fro throughout the whole earth, to show himself strong on behalf of those whose hearts are completely his." When I read these stories, I have confidence that God sees my circumstances, he cares for my safety, and I am not out of his reach.

**Challenge:** Do you feel like your values are at odds with those around you? Do you feel alone? Pray that God would bring you into contact with people who are like-minded, so that you can be an encouragement to one another. But while you wait, have confidence that you are not alone.

# I Am Second

There is little more inspiring to me, as you can tell, than hearing someone's story of how God has broken through their circumstances, let them know that he is there, and opened doors before them onto a new path forward. Well, imagine my joy when I discovered I Am Second! This non-profit organization devotes itself to sharing the stories of people who have experienced a breakthrough and now follow Jesus. They have produced more than 130 films that are available on their website and their YouTube channel. Here are some glimpses of some of my favorites:

RA Dickey, 2012 winner of professional baseball's famed Cy Young Award, tells of the moment he was turned down by the Texas Rangers right after college. During a pre-employment exam, they found a missing tendon in his arm. When the team manager delivered the news, Dickey said, "It was all I could do not to pummel him. But in that moment, I felt something like a wind, a feeling wash over me, and the feeling was, 'it's okay, I've got you.'" The subsequent years of his career were full of struggle, until the moment he nearly drowned in the Missouri River.  With nearly all his strength gone, losing his ability to fight the current, he wept and apologized to God for leaving his girls without a father. Suddenly he felt the river bottom under his feet, and felt a surge of adrenaline, and was able to make it to the river's edge. From then on, he made it his goal to "live the next five minutes well, whatever that meant." He began to imagine his famous pitch, the knuckleball, as a visual illustration of the life that God has for us. In order to execute a knuckleball, the pitcher needs to surrender the ball to the direction it needs to go. It reminds Dickey that he was holding on tightly to everything in his life, but to accept what God had for him, he had to open his fingers and let God have was Dickey was holding.

Brian "Head" Welch, of the rock band Korn, tells his story of the hard core, drug-infused, party lifestyle that was his as a member of the band. The band's success enabled him to have anything money could buy. In time, the drugs got in the way of his ability to raise his young daughter, especially once her mother had succumbed to addiction and was no longer in the picture. Out of the blue, Brian's real estate broker told him, "Listen, Brian, I don't normally do this. I'm not really sure how to say this, but I feel like this will mean something to you: 'Come to me, all you who are weary and burdened, and I will give you rest for your soul.'"(Matthew 11:28) Brian said that verse got his attention. Within a few weeks he found himself at his real estate broker's church, praying with people there and asking Jesus to come into his heart. He went home, sat his daughter down in front of the TV, and started doing drugs. He said, "Jesus, if you are real, you gotta take these drugs from me. Jesus, search my heart."  He describes the feeling of fatherly love filling his body.  It was so powerful that the next day, he threw away all his drugs, and decided to quit Korn and stay home with his daughter full time. "I tried everything to try to get pleasure out of this life. But Christ came in, and gave me the gift of understanding life, which is, everything was created by Christ, and for him, and we were created to be with him, and it's the most incredible feeling, because you're where you belong."

Danny Gokey, another musical artist, describes the struggles of growing up dealing with fear, always wanting to know, "God, are you with me?" His anxiety reached a peak before his appearance in the final section of American Idol Season 8. Thinking he was so worn out from anxiety that he was about make a fool of himself, he heard God saying to him, "Be still and know that I am God." Unable to make himself "be still", Danny looked up the Hebrew words, which were translated "stop striving." He discovered that the things he was hanging onto, asking God why, were the things that made him bitter and angry and were pulling him down. He found that once he let go of those things, God answered his prayers, and reinvigorated his soul with life again. His music started impacting people. He would receive letters from people who had been without hope, ready to end their lives, but they heard his music and didn't go through with it. Step by step, his career has prospered, as he daily leans toward Jesus, trusting in the fact that Jesus is enough.

Michelle Aguilar, winner of The Biggest Loser, tells the story of how she masked her pain with a smile, and comforted herself over the loss of relationship with her mother by filling the void with food. When Michelle was 18, her mother left her father and moved out. Michelle could not escape the thought that there must also be some reason her mother did not love her. When Michelle was accepted as a contestant for the show, she felt like God was telling her this would be the opportunity for a fresh start. Contestants needed to invite a spouse or a parent or a child as a companion in the show. Michelle's father suggested that Michelle should bring her mother. "It was so hard," Michelle said. "The other contestants had such strong relationships with their spouses, and here I was, with someone who was the source of my pain." The breaking point came when, in a challenge, Michelle's tooth was broken. "I couldn't smile. It was as if I lost my armor," said Michelle. "Laying there, in a complete state of brokenness, I gave it all to God. From that moment, everything began to change. I let it all go. I began to know that I could truly hand it over to God, who was, in every way, big enough to handle everything, and that he wasn't going to look at all my junk and run away. I discovered that me being in control was really me being out of control.  When I showed up for that finale, I was a changed person.  I really, truly began to walk in love and forgiveness for my mom. The scale was not going to define me."

**Challenge:** Search the I Am Second YouTube channel for White Chair videos of people familiar to you – I bet you will find a few stories that inspire you!

# Angels Watching Over Me

In my book This is Not Heaven, I mention that I keep a journal of the times God has stepped into my day and provided what was needed in the moment. Here is one story from that journal:

July 2001 – Stanley Park, Vancouver, Canada: We took a family vacation to Seattle, Vancouver, and Victoria. One day we rented bikes to ride around Stanley Park. Little did we know, the path was not a flat ride all the around the park. There were some hills, which would be a problem for our three and a half year old son, who had difficulty understanding how to stop the bike by pedaling backwards to brake. He had one speed: maximum velocity!

As we made our way around the park, and I got a taste of how much of a problem this could be, I saw a long slope ahead, followed by a railing next to what seemed to be a narrow path that dropped off to a steeper grade. Our son sped full speed toward it, completely unaware of the danger ahead. I screamed his name over and over at the top of my lungs, "Jordan, stop! Jordan, stop!" to no avail.

Then a miracle happened. Suddenly a man on a bike was stopped next to the railing. He slowly turned behind him and saw that Jordan was barreling toward him. He calmly and firmly reached out and took hold of Jordan's bike between the handlebars and held him there until I came up behind them. It was not until I could see the path that I could fully appreciate what could have happened without this man stopping Jordan where he did. It was quite a slope, barely manageable if taken from a full stop.

That five-mile bike path was quite a challenge for Jordan that day – this may not have been the only miracle! I have no doubt that without this man (was he an angel?) we would have been needing medical help on that hill for sure! Could God, in his wisdom, have allowed a painful accident in order to bring about something else that was needed in our lives that day? Absolutely. But in this instance, we are thankful that the plan for the day was a rescue!

And we know that in all things God works for the good of those who love him, who have been called according to his purpose.
(Romans 8:28)

**Challenge:** Do you have anxiety when it comes to your children's safety? In those moments, pray! Remember that God loves them even more than you do, and that he has the power to protect them and guide them. Ask for wisdom and strength and ability to provide what your children need. Ask for God to provide for them and protect them in any ways you cannot.

# American Miracles

Over the years, I have learned many ways that faith in God had a huge impact on the formation of the culture and government of the United States of America. So when I heard about Michael Medved's book The American Miracle: Divine Providence in the Rise of the Republic, I had to check it out! The stories he has assembled in this collection include evidence of how unlikely these events were, and the testimony of those at the time attributing them to divine providence.

What were these many acts of divine providence that were on the minds of the people living through them throughout our history? Here are a few that Medved recounts.

In 1620, the Mayflower pilgrims' landing was not where they had planned. They had been blown north. After a month of exploration, and harrowing trial and error, they sailed into the Plymouth harbor. And what a wonderful harbor it was! The harbor floor was deep enough for sailing ships, and the land formed a gentle slope that led up to a substantial hill with excellent sight lines in every direction. The area had been cleared of trees and used to grow corn until recently. The pilgrims quickly realized they had landed in a once thriving

Indian village called Patuxet, which they had seen on a map by explorer Samuel de Champlain produced in 1604. Knowing this, they were able to find caches of buried corn that de Champlain had described. They were saved! They thanked God and solemnly resolved to repay the rightful owners as soon as they could find them. But in time, they learned that an epidemic had taken the lives of 95% of those from this village and others nearby.

Second, though the pilgrims had been led to this ideal location, they still needed to learn how to survive there. Enter: Squanto. This native sole survivor of the village had only returned to Patuxet six months before the pilgrims arrived. He had been kidnapped fifteen years earlier and brought to London by explorers who taught him the English language and questioned him about the New World. After nine years in London, Squanto managed to gain passage home, only to be kidnapped again just before reaching Patuxet. This time he was taken to Spain. His captors intended to sell him and other captives as slaves, but the captives were ransomed by Spanish monks, in order to buy their freedom. After gaining back his strength, Squanto found his way back to Patuxet. Six months before the pilgrims arrived, Squanto entered his home village, only to find it void of any signs of life.

For a time he lived alone in the woods, then made his way to the nearest village, led by Massasoit. Massasoit was concerned for his people's safety, and wanted to make a treaty with the English settlers. Squanto facilitated those negotiations, and soon took up residence once again in his home village, to live alongside the pilgrims. He showed them how to catch eel that hid in the mud of local streams, and how to trap alewives, fast-moving fish that swam upstream in crowded schools once each year. Famously, he taught the pilgrims to plant five corn kernels surrounded by three fish to produce an abundant harvest, a technique he likely learned from the Spanish monks!

Stories of divine providence in Revolutionary war battles abound. Odds were stacked against the Continental Army. George Washington was quoted, "If I shall be able to rise superior to these [vulnerabilities to British attacks], and many other difficulties which might be enumerated, I shall most religiously believe that the finger of Providence is in it, to blind the eyes of our enemies."

One such instance of enemy blindness occurred on Dorchester Heights, above Boston Harbor. The British controlled the harbor and received continual reinforcements there. But one night, under cover of darkness, the Continental Army fortified the hill above the harbor with new artillery they had seized from the British. The weather that night was perfect for the task: a hazy fog settled above the British troops in the valley below, blocking their view of the fortifications taking place above their heads, in bright moonlight.

The British troops awoke to find the artillery looming overhead, and decided they had to fight or abandon their post. Both sides spent the day preparing for battle. That evening, the weather changed again: a fierce storm arose without warning, suddenly shattering window in the town and knocking down fences all around. The British ships in the harbor were incapacitated. The frozen slope below the fortification would be impossible for the British troops to scale. Instead, they extended an offer to General Washington: if they were allowed to withdraw without being fired upon or impeded, they would not burn Boston to the ground as they left.

Medved writes, "When the news spread, supporters of the patriot cause marveled at their good fortune. Washington freely acknowledged the intervening hand of God in stirring the fierce storm that facilitated his great victory."

Similar "meteorological miracles" occurred after the Battle of Long Island. Washington's army suffered the loss of likely more than a thousand men. They found themselves trapped at the far western corner of Long Island, with the British forces ahead of them, and the East River estuary behind them. Again, the weather turned; winds prevented the British ships from advancing to their position and firing upon them. British troops ahead watched for signs of a retreat, upon which they would strike when Washington's army was most exposed. Washington sent word to detachments in the New Jersey area to requisition every small boat with oars or modest sails to transport his army to a bold surprise attack. He directed a small contingent of the trapped army to stay where they were, making as much noise as possible to make it seem like no troops had left the area. The remaining troops were put to work through the night, moving the artillery and supplies toward the Brooklyn docks. Steady winds kept the British ships at bay. But morning light would expose those remaining at the docks, including those who had stayed behind to make noise but were now gathering to also retreat.

Incredibly, a dense fog appeared over Brooklyn, concealing the continued retreat until the last boat was across! Major Tallmadge was quoted, "In the history of warfare I do not recollect a more fortunate retreat. After all, the providential appearance of the fog saved a part of our army from being captured, and certainly myself, among others who formed the rear guard."

In another chapter, Medved details the many incidents in the life of George Washington that gained him the reputation of being "indestructible." As an aide to British General Braddock in the effort to take possession of French forts starting with Fort Duquesne, young Washington found himself a survivor of a day of carnage that left 977 of 1,459 soldiers killed or wounded. During the battle his horse was shot. He found another, which was also shot within minutes. His third mount managed to carry him through the remainder of the battle. Washington's hat was shot off of his head, and four other bullets penetrated his coat. Amazingly, none of these shots grazed his body even slightly. The providential protection of George Washington in this battle became legendary. His courage, founded in faith, inspired the nation.

Additional chapters on the Constitutional Convention, the Louisiana Purchase, the paths to statehood for Texas and California, and President Lincoln and the Civil War provide more evidence of God's hand in the life of the United States of America.

I love these quotes that precede the first chapter:

"I have lived, Sir, a long time, and the longer I live, the more convincing proofs I see of this truth – that God governs in the affairs of men. And if a sparrow cannot fall to the ground without his notice, is it probable that an empire can rise without his aid?" - Benjamin Franklin, remarks to the Constitutional Convention, June 28, 1787

"No people can be bound to acknowledge and adore the Invisible Hand which conducts the affairs of men more than those of the United States. Every step by which they have advanced to the character of an independent nation seems to have been distinguished by some token of providential agency." – George Washington, first Inaugural Address, April 30, 1787

**Challenge:** Read The American Miracle by Michael Medved. Visit the website for Wallbuilders.Com, owner of the largest private collection of American historical documents, and read the biographies and actual writings of people who are a part of early American history. Search for more stories of instances when God has intervened in the life of a nation – America is not the only one!

# Close to the Brokenhearted

The LORD is close to the brokenhearted, and saves those who are crushed in spirit. Psalm 34:18

When my grandmother passed away, it was a very difficult time for my mother. Full of sadness over missing her, and battling nagging thoughts about what else might possibly have been done for her, my mother's grief was overwhelming.

To ease the pain and provide some distraction, my mother decided to do some of the things my grandmother loved to do. One of those things was to go shopping. Ross was a favorite store to peruse for a new top or shoes or other treasures.

My mother entered the store full of sadness, missing my grandmother's presence in an activity they had shared many times. She wandered the aisles as she had so many times before, not really looking for anything, just putting one foot in front of the other.

As she turned into the home décor area, she caught sight of something, and was instantly filled with peace and comfort. Not only that, but she had the sense that my grandmother was at peace as well.

All alone on the shelf sat a garden stone bearing the image of an angel, with a fat little bird on her dress, and the word "Peace" etched on it. My mother was stopped in her tracks. The combination of an angel (a favorite thing that my mother collected) with fat little bird (a favorite thing that my grandmother collected) etched onto a garden stone (when my mother's favorite thing to do at home was to spend time tending her plants in the backyard) brought my mother the comfort she needed in that moment. She felt like it was a message from God just for her. She knew in that moment he felt her sadness. She knew in that moment my grandmother was in his trustworthy hands.

The next time she visited the store, she found a similar angel rock, again all by itself. This time the rock was with etched with the word "Faith." Such comfort my mother felt again, and her faith definitely grew!

**Challenge:** Think about a time when you felt God step into your circumstances and let you know he cared for you. Thank him for his comfort.

# #LetUsWorship

As I write this, we are approaching the one-year anniversary of the mid-March 2020 "15 days to stop the spread" of the coronavirus called COVID-19. Mask mandates abound, many American schools are still not back full time in person, and many adults are still working from home. Gathering places of all types are under varying specifications of restriction such as percentage of normal capacity, specified maximum capacity, and/or limited hours of operation, depending on orders issued by state governors.

California has been one of the most restrictive states in the nation when it comes to allowing churches to reopen for services in person. Governor Newsom's mandate even includes a ban on singing during worship services. California is also the home to a very large, renown, and Holy Spirit-focused church: Bethel Church in Redding, California. Bethel Music produces Christian worship songs that are sung around the world in Christian churches where contemporary music is a part of worship. Sean Feucht (pronounced FOYT) is one of Bethel's volunteer worship leaders.

Churches remained closed through Easter, then still closed through May. When protests erupted in multiple cities after the death of George Floyd on

May 26, the authorities instituted curfews and blocked off streets. June was a month of unrest. Even where streets were peaceful, it was hard to shake the feeling that injustice permeated all that was happening in our land. July 4th arrived. Few cities held fireworks displays due to the COVID shutdown. This is when I first started to see Sean Feucht coming up in my Instagram feed. He challenged people to sign a petition to "LET US WORSHIP," declaring that now more than ever, people needed God and each other, and we needed to gather and worship God and pray. On July 9th, with a few instruments, amplifiers, and microphones, he and his team gathered people to worship on the Golden Gate Bridge, and pray that God would open the gates of blessing in their state. The next day they worshipped in Huntington Beach, following a dream one of the team had about a multitude of people worshipping there and "so many being baptized that people had to turn and baptize the person behind them." Hundreds came to worship. Many prayed to receive Jesus, and were baptized in the Pacific Ocean. Some reported that they were healed of anxiety, depression, or other medical issues. Sean's team declared, "The church has left the building!"

Response was enormous. People across the country began following on Facebook and Instagram, praising God along with Sean's worship team as they live-streamed from wherever they were. Sean's team was open to going where they felt God leading them.

Next, they travelled to New London, CT and New York City. In New London they worshipped in an historic building where there were services held during the Great Awakening. In New York City they worshipped and baptized people in the Washington Square fountain. Afterward Sean posted on Instagram: "I had a dream a month ago about spontaneous baptisms happening in one of the most iconic places in the city: Washington Square Park. At the time, NYC was shut down and this fountain was turned off. But last week it came back on for the first time in months. After a crazy joyful worship set, [prayer for] racial reconciliation and a salvation call, we marched over to the fountain last night. The NYPD let us go for it, too! The dream became reality! Don't stop dreaming church!"

On July 22nd, the team went to Redding, then to a new city each day for the next five days: Pasadena, Bakersfield, Fresno, and Encinitas. The tour has continued since then, with stops all around the country. To Sacramento to worship on the steps of the state capitol. To Seattle, where protestors had held Capitol Hill and renamed it the Capital Hill Autonomous Zone (CHAZ). To Minneapolis, where the city burned after the death of George Floyd. To Madison, WI to worship at the state capitol, then to Milwaukee, then to Kenosha, where a recent shooting had been caught on cellphone video and made national news. On to Chicago, where 63 people had been shot the previous weekend. Sometimes, in the name of COVID restrictions, city officials blocked space where they planned to worship that evening. In that case, the team would move to a space nearby, declaring a "peaceful protest." They believed they had followed the Holy Spirit to each place where God wanted them to reach people, and they would let nothing stand in the way of their steadfast intent to worship God, to ask God for peace and healing for our land, and to save souls in every place where he had led them.

At this point, they have been going strong for eight or nine months, with a few breaks in between, and no sign of stopping! Read through Sean Feucht's Instagram feed and you will find stories of healing from hearing loss, people dropping their crutches and braces, leaving their wheelchairs, letters from people who say their lives have been restored in various ways, all because they were doing what Jesus said to do, which is to humble themselves like a little child before their Heavenly Father. (Matthew 18)

Is healing a common thing that happens in our American churches today? No. Does that mean we should be wary of claims of healing? Haven't some people collaborated to fake healing in worship services in order to get people to make donations? Yes, that has happened in some cases. I am no expert on this topic, but I will tell you how I approach it. Jesus healed people, and he sent his disciples out to proclaim the gospel and to heal the sick (Matthew 10; Luke 10), which they did. But the bible also says that many in Jesus' hometown of Nazareth had a hard time believing that he was the Messiah, and because of their unbelief, he did not perform many miracles there (Matthew 13:58). So I see that there is God's desire for healing and restoration for people, but I also see that unbelief can hinder healing and restoration. Also there may be many other factors in a situation that impact whether a person is healed or not, factors that are not apparent to me. I read the story of Jesus giving sight to the man blind from birth in John 9, and I realize that I need to open to possibilities in a situation that I might not expect. God's ways are higher than our ways. (Isaiah 55:8-9). So I examine the fruit of the lives of the people who are involved in the alleged healing, compare their words and actions to what the bible says, and over time, and with prayer for discernment, I decide whether I personally will believe that healings are taking place through them. All of this careful consideration is only to keep myself walking with Jesus in spirit and in truth...if people are faking healings, they will answer to God for their actions, not to me! And God does not approve of people deceiving one another!

I highlight what Sean Feucht is doing for one reason. He is a man who daily steps out in faith, believing that God will do what he says he will do. He expects to see God working. He has made space in his life for God to work, and get the glory. Sean Feucht does his part, for sure – he is not just sitting back and waiting for God to do it all. He makes himself available to God. He tells people about what he sees God doing around him. He fully embraces God's plan for our lives, as described in John 15. Jesus is the vine, and we are the branches. The life of the vine flows through us, and we bear the fruit. Jesus said, "Apart from me, you can do nothing."

**Challenge:** How might you get involved in what God is doing in the world around you? What do you see around you that breaks your heart? How could you use your time, talents, or resources to be the hands and feet of Jesus to people around you? Pray and ask God to lead you in what he would have you do.

# Full Reliance

Another interviewee of Eric Metaxas caught my attention this year. Her name is Bevelyn Beatty.

I love how Eric Metaxas always asks his guests about how they came to faith in Jesus, and made him the Lord of their life. Her journey was compelling.

Bevelyn is African-American. She was born in New York City, but grew up in North Carolina because her father brought her family there to avoid being charged with murder in New York. Eventually her father was cleared and went back to New York City. Bevelyn decided to make her way there as well. She attended college but did not take it seriously, and was eventually "kicked out." To make enough money to support herself in the way she wanted to live, she worked, but also had a "side hustle" to make ends meet. Even though her life was full of people she called friends, and she was able to make a life for herself so far, she was not happy.

One night she came home drunk from a party. She went into the bathroom, turned up the water so her roommate wouldn't hear, and cried. She thought about all the things she had: designer shoes, fur coats, any man she wanted. Nothing filled the emptiness she felt, nothing made her feel valuable or loved. She was miserable. She cried out to the Lord for help. But in the morning, she kept living the only way she knew how.

About two weeks later she was in jail for money laundering, waiting for her father to bail her out. She had been waiting for several days when she was visited by a woman she didn't know. The woman told Bevelyn about the night she had cried out to the Lord, describing details that only she and the Lord knew. Bevelyn was shocked! The woman went on to say that the Lord had told her Bevelyn would be released on the following Tuesday, and she needed to repent of her sins and surrender her life to the Lord because the path she was on would end in death.

Tuesday came, and Bevelyn was released. The woman had been right! Bevelyn was in awe, and terrified of getting caught doing anything illegal again. She knew she would have to give up her side hustle. In an interview that is available on YouTube, by Harvest Rock Church, she said, "I had been working since I was 14. I didn't ever not value the concept of work. I knew that if I need something, I gotta go out and get it. But my mentality was, by any means necessary, I'm gonna feed myself and I'm gonna figure out a way to survive. Because if you don't have family, and you don't have people to look out for you, you gotta do what you gotta do to take care of yourself, *so you think*...until you know Christ." She determined that she would have to live on just what she could make for honest work. She prayed, "Lord, I don't know how to do right, but I know when I'm doing wrong, and I'm going to make a decision right now to serve you."

For the next year, she made some different decisions. She stayed away from doing things that were illegal to get money, but still used men to get things she wanted, like money to pay a bill that wasn't quite covered, or for weed. She smoked weed regularly, including before church every Sunday, because it was normal in the world she was living in. She tried to do right.

One day, about a year after getting out of jail, Bevelyn was soliciting donations for the feminist organization she worked for, in front of Trump Tower on Columbus Circle. She approached a woman and tried to persuade her to make a donation. The woman listened to Bevelyn's pitch. When Bevelyn asked if her to donate, the woman said, "Well, you know, we could give money, but if the women don't know Jesus, it won't really make a difference." Bevelyn thought, "You know, you're right." The woman gave Bevelyn her card. Two weeks later, they had dinner, then started meeting for praise and worship on Saturdays. From there began a friendship between the two women, where Bevelyn learned more about how to have a relationship with Jesus, and about how important it is to grow in grace by spending time reading the bible and following what the Lord has said in his word. This friendship has been life-changing for Bevelyn. She sees God's hand in bringing them together, saying it is a miracle that she did not lose her card like she normally would in that two weeks before they had dinner!

About six months later Bevelyn visited her family in Charlotte. On the day she would return to New York, she smoked weed as usual, then returned her rental car and got a ride to the airport from a Hispanic woman. The woman had a picture of Jesus on her phone. Bevelyn said, "Hey, I have that same picture of Jesus on my phone!" The women spoke little English but they both were joyful about their shared relationship with Jesus. As she and the women went on and on about how they loved Jesus, Bevelyn felt like a phony because she had just smoked weed. She told the woman that she had a problem with weed, and she needed help, and asked the woman to pray for her. The woman agreed. She prayed in Spanish, so Bevelyn did not understand what the woman was saying, but she felt the power of Holy Spirit upon her. From that point on, she has never smoked weed again!

When Bevelyn talks about how life has changed for her, she says that the Lord has made her new. She passionately talks about how she has been delivered from a life of sin, manipulating people and stealing from them, comparing herself to others, needing to have the handbags, the shoes, and the labels that other people had around her, feeling constantly insecure, and depending on what people thought of her for a feeling of value. She was depressed then, but now she is joyful because she knows she is valued by the Lord, and he is providing for her needs. She says, "I realized I needed help, and I let him help me."

**Challenge:** Do you feel like it is all up to you to get what you need to survive? Like you have to take what you need or you will not have enough? God did not intend for you to live like that. He intends for us to use our strength and skills to do work that produces something that we can provide to others, and that others do work that produces something for us. He intends us to live in community, trading with those who can work, and sharing what we have with those who cannot work so that their needs are provided for. We are to live in a way that is pleasing to him, to love and honor him, to love and respect others, to help others in our work and in our communities. When we do that, he, our Heavenly Father, promises to provide what we need to live. He blesses the work of our hands. (Ephesians 2:10; Ephesians 4:8; 1 Timothy 5:8; Deuteronomy 15:10; Proverbs 13:4; Proverbs 18:9; Colossians 3:17) Is there some way in which you need to stop trusting in your own strength, to stop cutting corners, stop taking what is not yours, and start trusting in God to provide? Pray for his direction on how to do that today.

# Nazi Survivor

As I write this, it has been eighty years since Adolf Hitler found a way to uplift the weary and broken souls of the German people by vilifying a subgroup in their midst, setting in motion a murderous machine that expanded as far as France to the west and Russia to the east. The horrific example of the power of the state in the hands of an evil human has not faded with time. Daily, members of Congress, journalists, and political podcasters compare their political opponents to Hitler, and compare policies to those of Nazi Germany.

Likely the stories live on because we still have no idea how it could have been prevented. We are shocked that good people could have cowered in fear and cooperated in the abuse and murder of millions. We wonder how we would react if we had lived there at that time.

But my heart is encouraged when I hear stories from survivors who experienced God's provision in the midst of their persecution. One such survivor is Anita Dittman, and her story is told in her book, Trapped in Hitler's Hell. She was a young woman who lived in Breslau, Germany. Her mother was Jewish, her father was not. He abandoned his wife and two daughters when the pressure became too intense. Anita's sister was able to get papers to leave for London before Poland was invaded, but papers for Anita and her mother never came.

Anita and her mother were Jewish Christians. From the beginning of the war, their attitude was one that trials were an opportunity for trusting Jesus more. Their pastor was a man who did what he could to help Jews, whether they believed in Jesus or not. When pressure came to Breslau for Jewish students to be separated in the community, their pastor was able to find Anita a place to live with a woman in another town for a while where she could go to school. After many months, it became apparent that the woman was taking advantage of Anita's ration coupons and Anita was becoming malnourished. By this time, attention on Jews in Breslau had eased, so Anita was able to come home again. She was delighted to be reunited with her mother.

In the book she shares many stories of how the Lord provided for her and her mother. In the spring of 1942, Anita turned fifteen. Her mother was forced to work the night shift in a canning factory. They thanked God that while city after city around them boasted they were free of Jews, Anita and her mother still lived in the Jewish ghetto and had relative freedom. Non-Jews dared not come into the ghetto for fear of being labeled as sympathizers. Anita and her mother had enough food to eat, and still participated in services and other events with their church.

"It was a paradox," Anita said. "Just as I felt the most isolated, God would manifest his power and control over all of our circumstances. His watchful care and protection over all of us who believed on the name of Jesus would fill hundreds of volumes. His protection of Mother and me was just a tiny grain of sand on the giant seashore of his safety and love.

"I almost felt happy when the Gestapo ordered me to report to the canning factory for forced labor in the fall of 1942. Both Mother and I would work the day shift, and we thanked God that we could again spend our time together...the work was tedious and monotonous as we shredded onions and peeled carrots all day long...the onion fumes were so strong that our supervisor stayed away, and we were left alone to visit together. We prayed and talked and dreamed of better days ahead, and occasionally ate an onion when the hunger pangs became too severe."

By the spring of 1943, the tide was turning, and it was apparent Germany was losing the war. Hope rose with rumors that the concentration camps might be liberated by the Allies in the coming months. But there were more dark days ahead.

Anita and her mother, of course, had times when it was hard to take what God was allowing to happen around them. One of those times was when word came of what happened in the Jewish ghetto in Warsaw, Poland. Five hundred thousand Jews had been herded into the ghetto to starve to death. When they fought back, the Germans attacked with tanks, armored cars, artillery, and flame-throwers. Only five hundred Jews survived to tell about it.

At the factory that week, the mood was grim. Anita writes, "We could hardly speak to one another without choking back tears of grief and anger; even within the purest heart, bitterness raged toward the Nazis. Our faith was shaken and our hope dimmed. The atheists among us cursed, while the Jewish unbelievers withdrew into themselves. The religious Jews prayed harder and asked why. We Christians comforted one another and realized that some answers would only be available in heaven."

Anita shares how the trials changed her perspective: "God surely comforts the afflicted, but he afflicts the comfortable. Mother had been comfortable in her open-ended, believe-what-you-will religion. Now God was daily testing our faith and trust in him, and our walk with him was truly an adventure. Actually he moved and worked so fast in our lives that we often wished the adventure would slow down. God had stripped us of everything in life, yet we felt as if we had the wealth of a king. In fact, we did—the King of Kings. Someday we would taste all his glorious riches and wealth."

About this time, Anita fell ill with jaundice. Her supervisor at the factory began to scold her for being slow in her work. Anita and her mother were frightened because when workers could not work, they were in danger of being sent to a death camp. They prayed for wisdom for several days. During that time, Anita had a dream about her mother boarding a ship and sailing away to a death camp. Instead of fear, Anita was overcome with "a peace that passed understanding." She had the impression that no matter what happened, whether the ship arrived at the death camp, or sank on the way, her mother would be safe, and so would she.

That week they heard that Christian Jews in Breslau were still relatively safe, so her mother insisted that Anita visit the company doctor. Miraculously, instead of giving Anita a prescription for the death camp, the doctor sent her home for a few weeks to rest. "I'm told you're a good worker. We need good workers like you to rebuild the Reich and add to its glorious future. When you return, I'd better hear that you're working twice as hard."

During the third week of her four weeks at home, her pastor visited. By this time, it was apparent that Germany would lose the war, but Hitler would never give up. He said, "Anita, you and your mother are in danger. But never forget that Jesus is able to give you unexplainable peace, no matter what the circumstances. The apostle Paul wrote about that. In spite of his beatings, jailings, and shipwrecks, he always had joy and peace. He told us to rejoice always. Promise me you will remember that?" Anita said his visit breathed life into her, and she was able to gain strength for the difficult road ahead.

That Christmas, he was able to visit Anita and her mother again in their small apartment in the Jewish ghetto of Breslau. Again, his words would be etched in Anita's memory and recalled countless times in the coming months. "God is greater than all the combined evil of the Third Reich," he said. "He is in control of the war and in control of your lives, too. I feel he will preserve you and your mother, Anita, but you must be strong witnesses for him everywhere."

One morning in January of 1944, Anita looked up at the sky. It looked like it had in her dream, and she was filled with a sense of dread. Her mother told her she was being silly, and urged her to hurry up and dress for work. But soon the Gestapo came to the door to take her mother to a work camp.

Being left alone in Breslau to continue to work in the factory was nearly devastating to sixteen-year-old Anita. But her mother had slipped Anita her father's phone number, and it became an opportunity to heal that relationship. Also, since prisoners at her mother's work camp were able to receive weekly food packages, Anita put her lonely free hours to use gathering food to send to her mother. Anita says, "I survived on starvation rations for months, but never lost a pound, became sick, or missed a day of work. God just nourished me supernaturally in a way I will never understand."

Oh, the wild stories of God's provision that Anita shares in this book! One morning, Anita had a tremendous urge to send zwieback bread to her mother instead of her mother's favorite, pumpernickel. She sent it right away, and prayed that it would be delivered quickly. Later she received a postcard from her mother. Her mother had urgently prayed that day that Anita would send zwieback bread to help her recover from dysentery. The package had arrived in record-breaking speed!

Soon Anita's situation changed and she was no longer able to be in contact at all with her mother. In August, Anita was sent to a labor camp in Barthold, where she would dig ditches to protect the Germans from Russian tanks. Anita was able to send one last loaf of bread, with a note tucked inside, to let her Mother know what had happened, before she had to report to the Gestapo at the train station the next morning.  As the train rolled through the German countryside, she wondered if the farmers were aware that to the Nazis, their cattle was of more value than the lives aboard the trains that journeyed through their land. She wondered if they went to church on Sunday and prayed to the Jewish (and Gentile) God, but spurned the Jews. Anita and the other prisoners rode in silence, many too fearful to speak. Anita was thankful for the inner peace that gripped her, giving her "and indefinable assurance that God was in total control, not just of our lives, but of Germany, the Allied countries, and all the war-weary world."

She slept in a barn with many other women. They worked for ten hours a day, and were left to themselves in the evening, to settle down to sleep on a horse blanket on the barn floor, with a little straw for a mattress. She was thankful she was able to keep her bible, and was able to find encouragement for herself and the women who shared her fate.

Life there was very hard, but there were more miracles of God's provision, almost daily. I could write pages more, but I will let you purchase her book to read them! Except I will relay one more powerful story quickly.

At one point, Anita's leg was injured badly. The injury was very painful, and the wound became putrid. Anita became discouraged and cried out to God, asking why he had allowed this to happen, and why he was allowing her to go through such pain. But when a guard and would-be rapist was stopped in the evil act because he is nauseated by her disgusting wound, Anita rejoiced in the blessing of her injury that protected her from this attack!

I will spoil the ending and let you know that she obviously does survive, and is wonderfully reunited with her mother. Honestly, I'm leaving out many more wonderful stories – please, get her book and be encouraged!

**Challenge:** What would it take for you to adopt the attitude that trials are an opportunity to trust Jesus more? What would it take for you to be able to maintain hope in the face of such evil and injustice? Would you be able to see through your pain and focus on what God is providing for you, to lean into his presence where you are?

# Day One

I am not the only one in the world with the idea to collect "wild stories." Matthew West was moved by the letters he had received from people whose lives were impacted by his music, so he asked fans to submit their stories to him about what God had done for them. He received 40,000 responses!

One of them was from Josh Shushkey, who managed a Pizza Ranch restaurant in Worthington, Minnesota. Josh had grown up in a rough area, and had a rough home life. By age 17, he had made some bad choices, and found himself in prison for ten years for dealing drugs.

While in prison, Josh found God. When he was released, he made a commitment to show everyone that he had really changed, and he wasn't going back to who he used to be.

He applied for one job after another, but was not having success. One of his friends from church knew a couple who owned a Pizza Ranch restaurant. They took a chance on Josh, and offered him a part-time job in the back of the restaurant. He worked hard and kept a good attitude. Eventually he worked his way up to the position of manager.

Josh was interviewed by Brad Peterson of Life 96.5 Radio about how it happened that Matthew

West had written this song about his life. Josh said that when he heard about Matthew West asking for stories, "it was a God thing. I didn't usually go to Matthew West's website. When I saw he was asking for stories, I thought, "Why not, might as well." I thought he probably wouldn't read all of them, or someone else might read them." He pretty much put it out of his mind after that.

Then in January of 2015, he was at work with Christian radio playing in the restaurant as usual. He heard the song Day One for the first time. "I finished a sentence of it and I said, "Wait, how did I do that? I've never heard this before." I told people at work, "I think this song is about me, because God is telling me in my heart, 'This song is about you, man.'"

Soon afterward, Josh got a call from Matthew West confirming that yes, the song was about him!

Josh says, "People always ask me, 'Josh, why are you always happy? I tell them, 'I'm not dead and I'm not in prison. Life is good!' We all go through things. It doesn't have to be as extreme as mine, but through God, everything is okay, doesn't matter what the situation is. God will never give up on you, no matter what. He might shake his head at you, and be a little bit disappointed, but he's always there with you. And he lets you suffer sometimes so that you learn your lessons, but he never leaves your side, without a doubt."

The faithful love of the Lord never ends!
    His mercies never cease.
Great is his faithfulness;
    his mercies begin afresh each morning.
I say to myself, "The Lord is my inheritance;
    therefore, I will hope in him!" (Lamentations 3:22-24)

It's day one of the rest of my life
It's day one of the best of my life
I'm marching on to the beat of a brand new drum

Yeah, here I come
The future has begun
Day one
- Day One, by Matthew West

**Challenge:** Check out Matthew West's album, Live Forever, that has Day One and other songs he has written, based on the stories that fans sent him. Visit his YouTube page for songs that inspire you! Some of my favorites are: Strong Enough, More, Walking Miracles, Nobody, and The God Who Stays.

# What Difference Does It Make?

What is the point of pursuing a life of faith in God? Going to church? Spending time with Christians? What difference does it make if I do or don't?

I say, if you are all in, it makes a world of difference!

Now, don't get me wrong. I know God honors baby steps in the beginning, when we are getting to know him. A person can spend years in this stage. For some people who have lived through damaging relationships where they have been betrayed and trust has been broken, sometimes a good amount of time is needed to be able to heal and to become able to trust anyone.

But there comes a time when faith in God won't get you anywhere unless you are ALL IN. Half-believing that God will get you through tough times is a trap. Those times when you doubt, you'll think you have to fix your problem NOW, alone, and that will lead to trouble! Throughout the bible, we read that God's people were constantly losing sight of him and trying to do things on their own, at which point he would leave them to their own devices, as they wished, and let them experience the consequences. NO THANKS! I want to enjoy the benefits of the strong tower of safety that is mine, as I live in the way God wants me to live! It's a relationship, first and foremost. I will take the great adventure ahead that is planned for me, rather than some small story I might write on my own, filled with extra pitfalls that were unnecessary because I got out from under his wings. When faced with a problem, I have done my best to make a habit to STOP and TALK TO GOD!

What I mean by "being all in"? First, it means spending time reading or listening to the bible. I cannot emphasize this enough. The bible is God's primary form of communication. Through the bible, we get to know him. He promises to make it make sense if you ask. He gives us a hunger and a thirst to read more, as we grow to understand him better, as we see our value through his eyes. So much practical wisdom is available there, advice on attitudes about time and work and money, and relationships with the people in our lives. When we are in need, often God will guide us to just the passage we need to hear.

Vital encouragement for life is found in the bible as well. I can weather any storm, knowing that God sees all, he knows all, that pain has a purpose, and that he will make things right in the end. This is huge! I can trust that every slight or challenge I face will lead to just compensation and reward if I handle it with faith, strength, love and grace.

For me, here is the difference it has made:

I had what most would consider a good life before I accepted Jesus. I had a family and friends who loved me, good health, and good prospects for work. But in comparison to my life now, I was walking around in a grey, scarce world, a dog-eat-dog world. I worried if I would be able to pay the bills. I worried about sickness and accidents. I couldn't handle it if I thought my boss was unhappy with me, or my friend said something insensitive. All that has changed since I accepted Jesus, and started to follow him.

Now, when I'm worried about finances, I look at how God has provided for me and my family, just as he said he would. I remember past scarce moments and how he came through. I read scriptures that say "I am young and now I am old, yet I have not seen the righteous forsaken, nor their children begging bread." (Psalm 37:25) I pray and remind him that he says my job is to trust him and work well with others and do my best and give him glory, and his job is to place me where I'll be a help, and to bless that place with abundance. I stay open and alert to actions he may be prompting me to take, that will always be consistent with his word. He loves it when we lean on his promises and choose to follow his ways even when it's hard. When it's hard, we are being pruned like a fruitful branch, so we can bear more fruit! (John 15)

Now, when I'm worried about a relationship with another person, I do not consider myself a victim of their power over me. I am not driven by my need for their affection or affirmation. I can look at them as another human being that God has placed in my life, who has talents and choices and a role to play just as I do. We can work together and support one another, and benefit from each other's strengths and make up for one another's weaknesses. If those things are a mismatch, we can work through it, and perhaps one or both of us shift away or move on. Things in life change, we grow, we learn new things. We are in one place for a season, then move to another. What if that person is dangerous? Again, I have to conclude that God has allowed this for a reason. If I ended up with this dangerous person through my sinful choices, I confess them to God and ask for help and a way out. If this person is in my life through seemingly random events, I look for what God could be trying to do through my circumstances, and through theirs. Through it all, God is with me each moment, able to guide me through crises, because he is not surprised, and he knows what is needed to resolve it.

When I came to understand God's view of our lives, and began to replace my old ideas of how the world works with the idea that I was not alone, and this joyful and painful journey had purpose and meaning, everything changed for me. I had strength, and energy for the day. I was motivated. I enjoyed and appreciated people, and had more compassion. I was grateful. Joy was more intense, pain was less intense.

Listen, time is short. Life is busy and full of distractions. You don't have time to do a bunch of research on spirituality, a subject in our culture that is vague and generally full of impractical ideas that may or may not work. Let me give you the bottom line of my thirty years of reading the bible, experiencing a walk of faith and trust in God, and seeking out the experiences of others who are doing the same.

It's my sincere hope that you will say, "Wow, that's awesome! I want this too!" If you don't, I'll be sad, but I'll understand. We all have to make our choice. Our choice is valuable. That is why we have a choice.

So, the bottom line is this:

1. Christianity is an invitation to relationship with God, the Creator of the universe. He invites us to be a part of his (eventually) perfect family. He provides, protects, and guides. We use our strengths and talents he has given us to do the work he has for us to do, work that can be hard, but work that is our valuable contribution, and for which we will be honored, maybe not immediately sometimes, but always eventually. Others use their talents in the same way, in areas where we are weak. Because of this, all are honored and valued, and God is praised for bringing into existing this wonderful community.

2. In this life on earth, God hopes we will choose this path and begin to learn about how to walk it, with the bible and the Holy Spirit as out guides. We will experience the joy of love, goodness, beauty and adventure. We will also experience the pain of hate, evil, isolation, and death. In heaven, all evil is banished, and fear and doubt are replaced by perfect love, perfect acceptance, knowing and being known. What was broken will be restored. We will reign with the Father, the Son, and the Holy Spirit forever.

3. On earth, if we choose not to take this path, we live without the guidance and protection that God would like to give us. We live with more fear, because we believe that everything is up to us, and that we are victims of the people around us. We live with a mindset of scarcity, and are constantly in survival mode. If we have a lot of money, we can become proud and feel invincible, or we might feel that we never have enough, and we might be driven to find ways to extract more and more money from the people around us. In death, our choice is honored, and we are forever separated from the life we were offered. We spend eternity with those like us: "the cowardly, the unbelieving, the vile, the murderers, the sexually immoral, those who practice magic arts, the idolaters, and all liars—these will be consigned to the fiery lake of sulfur. This is the second death." (Revelation 21:8)

   **Challenge:** I hope you choose to say to God, "If you're real, show me. Make your words in the bible make sense to me. Show me what you are doing in the world around me. Help me know you, and walk with you."

# Mission: Possible

In the forty days after his resurrection, Jesus appeared to his followers on various occasions, showing himself to be alive. His last words to them before he ascended to heaven were, "You will receive power when the Holy Spirit comes on you; and you will be my witnesses in Jerusalem, and in all Judea and Samaria, and to the ends of the earth." (Acts 1:7)

This is also our assignment. We are to be his witnesses.

What do witnesses do? They see something that has happened, and then they tell others about it. They testify to the truth about what they have seen.

This is it. This is our job.

So how do we do it?

Number one: We have to be looking. If Jesus did something miraculous in your life, would you see it? Would you be able to tell? Or would you immediately dismiss it as the result of some natural event? Our culture today looks almost exclusively for material answers to problems, assuming the problems are naturally caused and can only be solved by scientific research and reallocation of resources through law and policy. Is there room in your worldview for miracles?

By all means, be skeptical. There are plenty of people out there who want fame and attention, who may be telling a tall tale for personal gain. But make sure your mind is open to the possibility of miracles, or you won't be able to see those that happen right in front of you. Your mind will rationalize all the wonder away, and you will never be able to have the full relationship with your Creator that you were meant to have.

Number two: we have to tell the story of what we have witnessed. This takes courage. Following Jesus is an adventure! And he's got your back. So when you find yourself in a situation with a story to tell, and someone in front of you that needs to hear it, be brave, be calm, and speak the truth, in a way that shows your concern for them. That person's life could be changed for the better because you were willing to share your story. God will see and be pleased, and you will be rewarded!

I hope that you have been encouraged and inspired by the stories in this book, as I have. I hope that these stories will help you see your value, help you find your purpose, and most of all help you to live life as it was designed to be lived. I pray that you find yourself better prepared to engage in the adventure ahead.

Take the leap of faith, my friends! Then come back and tell me your wild stories!

# Prayer for Salvation

Lord, I confess to you that I have tried to build a life on my own without you, my Creator. I confess that I have not honored you in my life. I humble myself before you now, and thank you for the life you have given me, all the talents you have given me, and all that you have provided for me this far.

I see that I am a sinner, that I have been selfish and self-serving, and that you are calling me to a life that is different. Thank you for showing me that you have a different plan for my life, one in which I will fulfill all of the potential you have for me, in which I will use my gifts to bring you glory instead of myself, and in which I will find the joy and peace that you have meant for me.

Thank you, Lord Jesus, for shedding your blood in payment for my sins, past, present, and future. Thank you for your mercy on me, enabling me to step forward from this day on, walking in your grace and provision, showing me the new life you have for me, one day at a time.

Lead me each day, Lord Jesus. Be my shepherd. Let me hear your voice through your word. When I am joyful, I will praise you. When I am troubled, I will turn to you. When I am afraid, I will trust that you have my life, and the lives of those I love, securely in your hands. When I am tempted to sin,

I will remember that you have something better for me, and I will look for the way of escape that you have promised to provide for me. Thank you for your promise to lead me and guide me, and to provide for my needs. Be glorified through my life, and teach me to walk in your ways.

Amen.